# EMPEROR HIROHITO

The Emperor                    The Empress

# EMPEROR HIROHITO

## A Pictorial History

published by
**KODANSHA INTERNATIONAL LTD.**
Tokyo, New York & San Francisco
in collaboration with
**SHUKAN GENDAI**

ACKNOWLEDGMENTS
The compilers and publishers are grateful to the following for permission to reproduce the photos in this book: the Imperial Household Agency; Kyōdō News Service; and Kodansha Ltd.

*Distributors:*
*UNITED STATES: Harper & Row, Publishers, Inc., 10 East 53rd Street, New York, New York 10022. SOUTH AMERICA: Harper & Row, International Department. CANADA: Fitzhenry & Whiteside Limited, 150 Lesmill Road, Don Mills, Ontario. MEXICO & CENTRAL AMERICA: HARLA S. A. de C. V., Apartado 30–546, Mexico 4, D. F. UNITED KINGDOM: TABS, 7 Maiden Lane, London WC2. EUROPE: Boxerbooks Inc., Limmatstrasse 111, 8031 Zurich. AUSTRALIA & NEW ZEALAND: Book Wise (Australia) Pty. Ltd., 104–8 Sussex Street, Sydney 2000. THAILAND: Central Department Store Ltd., 306 Silom Road, Bangkok. HONG KONG & SINGAPORE: Books for Asia Ltd., 30 Tat Chee Avenue, Kowloon; 65 Crescent Road, Singapore 15. THE FAR EAST: Japan Publications Trading Company, P. O. Box 5030, Tokyo International, Tokyo.*

*Published by Kodansha International Ltd., 2–12–21 Otowa, Bunkyo-ku, Tokyo 112 and Kodansha International / USA, Ltd., 10 East 53rd Street, New York, New York 10022 and 44 Montgomery Street, San Francisco, California 94104. Copyright © 1975 by Kodansha International Ltd. All rights reserved. Printed by Toppan Printing Company, Tokyo.*

*LCC 75–21950*
*ISBN 0–87011–266–x*

*First edition, 1975*

# Contents

The chrysanthemum, native to China but introduced to Japan during the Nara period (710–784), has long been prized by the Japanese for its purity and elegance. The crest shown above—a double flower with sixteen petals—was officially adopted as the Japanese imperial emblem in 1889, but historians have traced the first appearance of the "imperial chrysanthemum" to the reign of Emperor Gotoba (1183–1198).

PRESENT

1. *Preceding page*: an informal shot of the Emperor at his villa in Nasu.

2. The Emperor and Empress in the front garden of the palace.

2

3-5. *Above left*, the imperial couple look through an old photograph album at the time of their golden wedding anniversary. *Below left*, the Crown Prince's children—Princess Nori, Prince Hiro (center), and Prince Aya—play bagatelle, to the amusement of their parents (seated left), the Emperor, the Empress, and Prince and Princess Hitachi. *Above*, a recent photograph of the Emperor and Empress in the east garden of the palace, now open to the public.

6-7. The Emperor in his office (*left*)—the Chrysanthemum Room of the Outer Palace. The Empress sometimes accompanies him on his way there (*above*). 15

8-12. The Emperor and his scientific interests. An acknowledged expert on marine biology, he spends part of each week at his laboratory (*above* and *bottom right*). His first discovery of a new marine specimen (*Sympasiphaca imperialis Terao*) is shown here; this he found at the age of seventeen near the imperial seaside villa, where the Emperor and Empress are pictured on holiday (*below*). The Emperor also enjoys tramping about his country estate looking at plant life.

13-14. The Empress is an accomplished artist. Now studying with Seison Maeda, one of the greatest living exponents of the traditional Japanese style, she has held various exhibitions of her work, has published a collection of paintings, and occasionally designs patterns for her kimonos. The Empress, sketchbook in hand, is seen in a seventieth-birthday portrait (*right*).

15-17. On a brief trip to the northern island, Hokkaido, in 1968, the imperial couple found time to inspect the local flora (*left*). Back four years later to open the Winter Olympics, well muffled against the cold, they are shown *below* visiting a zoo in Sapporo. The portrait *overleaf* was taken in front of the new Imperial Palace on the Emperor's sixty-eighth birthday.

18-22. Aspects of the new Imperial Palace: *above left*, the central courtyard; *above*, the Chowa-den Hall. In the *bottom row*, from left, are the Hōmei-den—the largest room in the palace, used for state banquets and parties celebrating the Emperor's birthday and the New Year; the Pine Room, used for the annual presentation of cultural awards and receiving ambassadors and foreign ministers; and the South Corridor of the Chowa-den, where guests wait before proceeding to the main lobby. The entire palace was completed in 1968 at a cost of roughly $36 million.

23-26. *Above left*, Nijū Bridge—the main entrance to the palace—is used by the Emperor only on state occasions. *Below* is his private residence, where the Empress has a small rose garden which she personally looks after. The Emperor is an avid television fan (*above*)—one of many indications that, far from being shackled by tradition and cut off from ordinary life, he is in good touch. Another is his policy, begun in 1947, of opening part of the palace to well-wishers on the second day of the New Year, when he appears several times during the day to wave and exchange greetings from a balcony. About 60,000 people attend each year (*overleaf*).

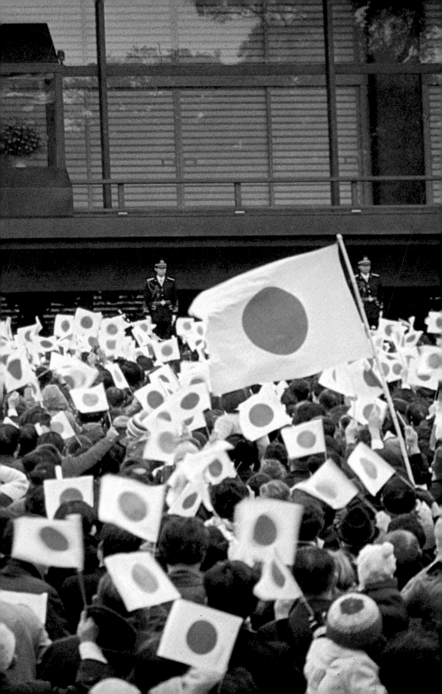

27-30. Each spring and fall, the Emperor holds a party in the Akasaka Imperial Gardens for representatives of the people and foreign diplomats (*left* and *bottom right*). *Bottom left*, he receives the gold-winning Olympic women's volleyball team in 1972, and attends a reunion with former classmates (*below*).

31. The Emperor and his family in January, 1975.

# PAST

1. *Preceding page*: the Emperor and Empress with their first child, Princess Teru, who was born in 1926; she died at the age of thirty-five.

2-3. The Emperor as a baby (*opposite*). Born at 10:10 P.M. on April 29, 1901, he weighed about six and a half pounds. *Below right*, Hirohito at eight months.

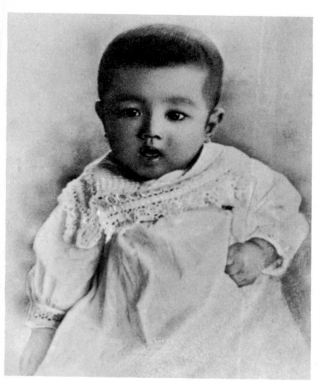

4-11. *Clockwise from above left:* Emperor Hirohito at three; at five, dressed in kimono; in 1908, when he entered the Peers' School; the Empress aged one (she was born in March, 1903, the eldest daughter of Prince Kuni); the Empress at four with her younger sister Nobuko, and *below,* six years later, dressed for the New Year; the Emperor, aged twelve, wrestling with one of his chamberlains; and on a hike in 1911 (his large Kodak was a present from his father).

12-17. *Above left*, the Emperor at twenty-one; *middle left*, playing golf with the Prince of Wales in Tokyo, 1922; and on the beach near his seaside villa (front, second from right). The portrait (*center*) was taken shortly after his return from Europe in 1922. *Above*, the Empress in 1923, a year before she married, and *below* with her family just before her wedding (seated in front).

18-20. *Left*, the imperial couple with their first-born child in 1926 at the Akasaka Detached Palace (now the Guest House), where they lived at the time. *Above*, they are pictured in the same residence in 1925 (the Empress's white grand piano is still there). *Top*, the Emperor aged twenty—two months before becoming Regent in place of his ailing father.

41

21-24. *Opposite above*, riding was one of the Emperor's favorite sports as a young man. He is also shown trying out his skis (*opposite below*) in the garden of the Fukiage Palace, 1931, and playing tennis with the Empress (*above*). At *left*, the Empress two months before her marriage. **43**

25-29. *Left*, the Emperor and Empress in traditional Heian-period dress at the time of his formal accession, November 10, 1928. *Bottom row*, from left: the Emperor—a marine biologist—in his laboratory in 1925; receiving the salute of American tennis champions at an exhibition match in the same year; and with the Empress and his daughters in 1933.

30-32. *Opposite left*, the Empress with Crown Prince Akihito, aged one, in 1934, and with three of her daughters in a Girl's Festival portrait five years later (*left*). *Above*, the imperial family in 1939 (front row, from left: Princess Taka, the Emperor, Crown Prince Akihito, and Prince Hitachi; back row, from left: the Empress, Princess Suga, Princess Teru and Princess Yori.

47

33-36. *Left*, a famous portrait with General MacArthur on September 27, 1945. *Above*, the Emperor signing the new Constitution in November of the following year, and visiting war orphans (*right*).

37-41. The Emperor is shown *opposite* with the Crown Prince at an athletic meet in 1946, riding in 1949 (*above left*), and inspecting marine specimens on his boat in 1952 (*above right*). At *left*, the Crown Prince with his English teacher, Mrs. Vining, and other students (the Prince is on the far left); and *below*, the Empress in 1947 with chickens she raised at the Fukiage Palace.

42-47. The picture (*left*) is of the Crown Prince and Princess just after their marriage on April 10, 1959. *Above*, the imperial family attending a garden party in 1965—from left, Princess Takamatsu, Prince Takamatsu (the Emperor's brother), the Crown Princess, the Crown Prince, and the Emperor and Empress. *Below left*, the Emperor opening the International Conference on Interparliamentary Union in 1960; presenting the Japan Academy awards (*below right*); with the Empress at a memorial service for the war dead (*bottom left*); and (*bottom right*) at a garden party in 1966 (from left, Prime Minister Satō, the Emperor, and Shigeru Yoshida—a leading postwar statesman).

48-53. *Clockwise from above*: the Emperor and Empress examining a rare piece of lunar rock; being greeted by wrestlers before a sumo tournament; at Ueno Zoo, with the pandas presented by the Chinese government; talking with actors at an NHK television studio; congratulating the Japanese women's expedition that scaled Mt. Everest in spring, 1975; and visiting the wild-duck preserve owned by the imperial family.

54

54. In 1921, when the Emperor was still Crown Prince, he made a six-month tour of Europe. It was the first time an heir to the Japanese throne had ever been outside Japan, and the Emperor remembers the journey fondly. "Until then,"

he says, "I was only a bird in a cage." The picture shows the young Crown Prince riding in an open carriage with King George V through the streets of London on May 9, 1921.

55-58. *Opposite above,* a close-up of Crown Prince Hirohito with King George V, and, *opposite below,* his arrival at Portsmouth. His visit included a tour of the British Museum (*left*) and an informal meeting with Lloyd-George, the British Prime Minister, at Chequers (*below*).

59-61. *Left*, the Crown Prince on a visit to Edinburgh; inspecting guardsmen at Victoria Station (*above*); and at an air display, where he met the Duke of York.

62. The Empress photographed in April, 1933, at the age of thirty. This is the first color photo taken in Japan. It was done with a Kodak camera and Kodak film, and the Empress chose this particular kimono because blue—or variations of this color—reproduced best in color film of the day.

# AFFAIRS OF STATE

1-4. *Preceding page*: in fall 1971, the Emperor made his first European trip since the war; the Emperor and Empress are shown at a banquet given by the President of the German Federal Republic. *Above right*, Emperor Hirohito greets President Ford in 1974 at the Imperial Palace and, *below,* at a special welcoming ceremony in the garden of the Guest House. *Overleaf,* President Ford—the first incumbent President to visit Japan—gives a speech at his return banquet in the Guest House.

5-9. With members of the British royal family: Queen Elizabeth II and the Duke of Edinburgh on their visit in May, 1975 (*above left*); Prince Charles, in Japan for the Osaka International Expo, 1970 (*middle left*); and Princess Margaret and Lord Snowdon in September, 1969 (*below left*). Queen Elizabeth—the first reigning British monarch ever to set foot in Japan—was shown a demonstration of *kemari* (traditional court football) at the Kyoto Imperial Palace (*left*). *Above*, a scene from the return banquet given by Her Majesty at the British Embassy.

10-15. *Top row*, from left: with the late King Feisal of Saudi Arabia at the Imperial Palace in 1971; at a banquet in honor of Princess Alexandra and her husband in 1961; and with Princess Beatrix of the Netherlands in 1963.

*Bottom row*, from left: greeting President and Mme. Marcos of the Philippines at Haneda Airport in 1965; with King Baudouin and Queen Fabiola of Belgium at the Imperial Palace in 1964; and with Secretary-General U Thant in 1970.

16-19. *Above left*, Emperor Hirohito greeting President and Mme. Tito of Yugoslavia at Haneda in 1968. A year later, the astronauts Collins, Aldrin, Sheppard, and their wives were presented to the Emperor (*above*). Sent as special envoys from the President of the United States, they were the first non-Japanese to receive Cultural Awards. At *left*, the Emperor welcomes President Mobutu of the Congo in 1971 and, *right*, is shown with the King of Malaysia at Haneda in 1964.

20-23. *Opposite above*, the Emperor and Empress arriving at the Elysée Palace during their European trip of 1971; *bottom*, in an open carriage with Queen Elizabeth and, *left*, at a banquet in Buckingham Palace. *Below*, a scene from the banquet given by the King of Belgium in Brussels.

24-28. Among the Emperor's annual duties are the Imperial Poetry Ceremony (*above left*) and the presentation of Cultural Awards —in this case, to Professor Ishihara of Johns Hopkins University (*left*); both occasions are held in the Pine Room of the palace. At *top right*, the Emperor and Empress are seen at the Ise Shrine; the shrine is sacred to the imperial ancestors. *Above*, the Empress, as Honorary Chairman of the Japan Red Cross, presents the annual Nightingale Awards. And *overleaf*, the Emperor launches the Tokyo Olympics of 1964—an event that focused worldwide attention on a new Japan.

29. A moment's pause from a demanding job as Emperor Hirohito and his wife stroll quietly along a path near the palace moat.

# A Personal Impression

OSANAGA KANROJI

I do not really remember just what month or year it was when I first met the present Emperor, but he was still a very small boy, known by his youthful name of Prince Michi.* I seem to recall that he was playing happily with his younger brother Prince Atsu (later Prince Chichibu) in the garden. Or maybe the two of them were sitting inside looking at a picture book. Whichever it was, I don't suppose it makes too much difference. I do remember quite clearly, though, that on this first meeting he struck me as a charming, refined-looking child. Like his father, his complexion was rather dark, but he had a friendly, intelligent face, and the eyes beneath his thick eyelashes were calm and bright. He resembled his father, but his rather long face also reminded me of his grandfather, Emperor Meiji.

I remember being deeply moved by the idea that one day—at the time it seemed an infinitely remote point in the future—this child would be the Emperor. Not long after that I became one of his attendants, and remained in his service until May, 1959, when I resigned from the position of Chief of Ritual. In these seventy years, the little boy I first knew has grown up and lived through more than one could easily write or tell. He is old now, and his hair is more gray than black.

I myself am ninety-five, but that first memory has remained so vivid that, even now, it's the boy's face that comes to mind

* The author is honorary director of the Meiji Shrine. Born in 1880, a former count and a schoolmate of Emperor Taishō, he served in the Imperial Household Agency for seventy years as Chamberlain, Chief of Ritual, and in other capacities.

whenever I think of him. And though I have seen the Emperor many times since I left the Imperial Household Agency, my first impression has never altered. Indeed, I know no one else who has changed so little over the past seventy years, and I have often asked myself why.

Working quietly and steadily at his scientific research, living peacefully among the birds and flowers at his country villa, happily doffing his hat to his people, unaffected by pomp and utterly unable to be ostentatious—the Emperor is a model for the nation as a whole.

Now, four years after his journey to Europe, he and the Empress are making their first visit to the United States, and they go with the earnest hope of contributing to international goodwill and peace. Those who have had the privilege of meeting the Emperor have invariably come away impressed with his warmheartedness, his open and unassuming nature. As for myself, it has been the joy of my life to be able to serve under such a considerate and gentle man.

# Monarchies and Republics

KENTARŌ HAYASHI

Before World War II, the Japanese propaganda line was that Japan's "national polity" (*kokutai*) had no counterpart in any other country in the world.* What it meant, in effect, was that the Emperor of Japan, unlike monarchs in other nations, was a sacred being descended from the sun goddess. This idea was largely a matter of government policy, and even then there were not many intellectuals in Japan who really believed it—least of all the Emperor, whose own attitude could never, in all honesty, be called ultranationalistic. One suspects, indeed, that for him nothing could have been more natural, more in keeping with his own feelings, than to announce after the war that he was a human being and not a deity.

There are about a hundred and fifty countries in the world today, and the great majority of them are republics, there being no more than twenty or so monarchies. There is a reason for this: monarchical systems are peculiar to countries with long histories, and more than half of the nations of the world today have come into existence since the end of World War II. In general, whenever a colony acquires independence, it sets up a republican system. The classic example is the United States, but the countries of Central and South America also adopted presidential systems when they freed themselves from Europe, and the nations that have become independent since the war are nearly all republics.

The essential difference between a monarchy and a republic is that the position of the head of state is hereditary in one and

* The author is President of the University of Tokyo.

not in the other. This is a completely separate question from whether a country is democratic or not. There are, of course, monarchies in which the government is autocratic, but in the more advanced nations there is democratic, parliamentary government within the monarchical system. In contrast, many of the developing countries, where strong centralization of authority is needed, have difficulty maintaining a democratic system, and government is to all intents and purposes dictatorial, even though the countries regard themselves as republics. In the self-styled "socialist countries," the system is invariably called "republican," but actual government is in the hands of the communist party.

Japan, like several of the western European countries, should be classed as a constitutional monarchy, for the Emperor "reigns but does not rule." Government is carried on by a cabinet elected by the Lower House of the Diet, and the Emperor has no power whatever to interfere in political affairs.

As a general rule, democracy develops within a governmental framework, and as it develops, the position of the monarch becomes more, rather than less, stable. This phenomenon began in seventeenth-century England and has continued to develop ever since. In this sense, democracy is not a system theoretically devised, but rather a natural result of historical evolution.

From the time of the Meiji Restoration until the end of World War II, the Emperor of Japan had enormous sovereign rights, as enumerated in the Constitution of 1890, but in fact it was rare indeed for the Emperor to assert his personal authority. After the war, Japan acquired a democratic system of government, and the Emperor's authority was reduced to as little as, if not less than, that of the English crown.

If monarchy and democracy can exist side by side, then what is the purpose of retaining the monarchy? One answer, I think, is seen in the postwar Japanese Constitution, which states that "the Emperor is the symbol of the Japanese nation and of the unity of the Japanese people." From the viewpoint of constitutional law, this is the earliest use of the world "symbol" to describe the monarch's role. True, under the Westminster Code employed in the British Commonwealth, the sovereign of England is described as a "symbol," but here it is not a ques-

ion of a monarch in his own nation, but one presiding over a
confederation of sovereign states. The use of the term "symbol"
in the Japanese Constitution is unique, and at the same time it
seems peculiarly fitting for the role of the ruler in a constitu-
ional monarchy.

From the beginning, nations have traditionally been governed by monarchs, and republicanism confined to small city-
states. Furthermore, throughout much of history, monarchy
*meant* monarchy, in the sense that a single ruler actually
governed his realm. Indeed, the rights of sovereigns during the
sixteenth and seventeenth centuries were so broad that it was
known as the age of absolute monarchy. In later times, the
rights of the people gradually expanded, and there developed
a strong resistance to monarchical authority. The French
Revolution was a result, and a number of similar uprisings
replaced the monarchical system with a republican one. This
did not, however, always entail the abolition of the monarchical structure. Today, in England, the Benelux nations, and
several of the nations of northern Europe—all of which are
among the most democratic countries in the world—monarchy
not only survives, but is extremely stable.

Rousseau, who is called the spiritual father of the French
Revolution, wrote of the "social contract," but a nation,
ultimately, is not created in accordance with the well-laid plans
of men. It is the product of long historical growth, during
which a people comes to share a common environment and a
common culture. Whenever men gather into a group, however, a political system appears, and together with politics, there
develop conflicts of interest and power struggles that threaten
the integration of the people. In the past, many a monarchy
has come to grief through excessive involvement in political
affairs.

It would appear, on the whole, that democracy cannot
survive long unless there is a certain national unity. In England,
during the seventeenth century, a republican system came into
being, but in no time the people were clamoring for the restoration of the monarchy. They considered, in effect, that this
essential unity could best be preserved by a hereditary king. At
the same time, the English took steps to limit the ruler's involvement in politics, and the English monarch gradually be-

came a nucleus of spiritual unity completely removed from the nation's political activities. Having no written constitution, the English do not refer to their sovereign in writing as a "symbol," though this is precisely the role that the king (or queen) plays.

In Japan, the legal definition of the Emperor as a "symbol' is new, but "symbol" would have been an accurate description of the Emperor's status since ancient times. As a nation, Japan is unusual in that it has always consisted of one more or less homogeneous race occupying the same territory. From the beginning, the imperial family has held sovereignty over the country, and its authority has never been seriously challenged. At the same time, since the ninth century, the imperial family has taken no direct part in national politics, but has instead stood well above the fray as the Fujiwara family, the Taira and Minamoto clans, the Ashikaga, Toyotomi Hideyoshi, and the Tokugawa shoguns rose and fell as the active rulers of the land. The imperial family has consequently survived as the highest symbol of authority in the nation. And it is fitting that the Emperor, with no political authority, but with a spiritual prestige founded solidly on history and tradition, should serve as the symbol of unity among the Japanese people.

It should be kept in mind, too, that the Japanese imperial family has more often promoted progress than hampered it. When it was decided to overthrow the Tokugawa government and create a new Japan, the process through which this was accomplished was not revolution, but a "restoration" of power to Emperor Meiji. In the course of this event, the Tokugawa family, though themselves the chief losers, voluntarily surrendered their authority to the Emperor, and the transformation to a new system was effected with a minimum of internal strife and bloodshed.

In the 1930's, when the Japanese military took control of the government and carried the nation into World War II, Emperor Hirohito was forced by the traditions of constitutional monarchy to abide by his government's decisions. Later, however, when the government proved incapable of functioning in the face of defeat, the Emperor, who had personally opposed the war throughout, decided to proclaim Japan's surrender. This in itself was an important contribution to the subsequent peaceful democratization of the nation.

# The Emperor's Daily Life

On April 29, 1975, Emperor Hirohito celebrated his seventy-fourth birthday. Born in the first year of the twentieth century, he has led a life that in many ways is a history in miniature of our period.

The Emperor has been on the Japanese throne longer than any of his predecessors. According to his doctors, the secret of his longevity is simply the regularity of his life and the care he takes to avoid any form of excess. Though now quite gray, for the past few years he has suffered no illness worse than an occasional light cold. And if people have noticed that he sometimes looks a little unsteady on his feet, this is because of his nearsightedness, of which he is so conscious that he walks with great care to avoid stumbling. He neither smokes nor drinks, his own explanation being that as a child he became ill after having some of the sweet saké customarily served in Japan to celebrate New Year's Day, and consequently lost any taste for alcohol.

The Emperor's day begins at seven in the morning. Apparently he rises earlier, but refrains from leaving his room to avoid disturbing those who wait on him. At seven on the dot he presses a buzzer by his bed to let the attendants in the next room know that he's up.

His bedroom, which no attendant is allowed to enter in his presence, is in the Western style, with an ordinary bed and red carpeting on the floor—one of many marks of a taste for certain Western ways acquired on his trip to Europe as Crown Prince, fifty-four years ago. (The Fukiage Palace, which is the Emperor's private residence, has only one room done in Japanese style, this being the Empress's own sitting room.) A taste equally universal—but presumably natural, not acquired—is his preference for wearing his oldest and most comfortable suits at home, often to the mild bewilderment of those around him. Being careless of his dress, he tends to leave things where he took them off, prefers his suits to be one shade or another of gray, dislikes brown, wears suspenders, and is not in the least dismayed that the sleeves of some of his favorite undress suits have gone shiny with wear. Predictably enough, it is the Empress who selects a tie to match whatever suit he has on when he goes out. . . .

The Empress is thought to arise around six in the morning. After washing, she joins her husband in the living room, where they read the newspapers and watch television until breakfast: the breakfast menu always includes bread, oatmeal, eggs, and a vegetable salad, with milk brought from the imperial dairy farm in Takanezawa, Tochigi Prefecture.

The Emperor subscribes to the three leading national newspapers and to most of the larger Tokyo papers. Occasionally he glances at one of the weekly magazines, though this is not part of his regular reading. Perhaps the most revolutionary change in the Emperor's habits for years came with the introduction of television, which he values as a means of keeping himself informed of affairs and fashions outside the palace. Moreover, like millions of other Japanese, he admits to watching the NHK "home drama" serial that comes on for a quarter of an hour every weekday at 8:15 in the morning; and as a keen follower of sumo wrestling, he is glued to the television set each afternoon of a tournament, though he only allows himself the last hour of each day's matches, owing to other work. He also watches the news, and has sometimes had court attendants make videotapes for him of special events such as the Apollo moon-landing.

At ten, the Emperor leaves for his office in the Outer Palace. When the weather permits, he walks to work, which takes about ten minutes. The Empress invariably sees him off at the bottom of the front steps, bowing politely to him as he lifts his hat in response, then watching until he starts to disappear round a corner about fifty yards away, when she bows again; at this point the Emperor always turns and waves his hat to her. This little family ritual has gone on throughout the fifty years since they were married. Nowadays, however, the Empress sometimes walks along with him and speaks to some of the volunteer workers who come every day to care for the garden.

A pile of documents invariably awaits the Emperor at his office, and at times he takes papers home with him to go over in the evening. His official duties, which are prescribed in Articles Six and Seven of the Constitution, are numerous and varied. They include promulgating constitutional revisions, ordinary laws, and regulations decided upon by the government; convoking the Diet into session; dissolving the Lower House when the government so requests; announcing elections for the Diet; endorsing appointments of ministers of state and other high officials; endorsing the credentials issued to plenipotentiaries, ambassadors, and ministers; endorsing amnesties, special pardons, reductions of sentences, stays of execution, and reinstatements for persons pardoned or paroled; conferring honors and bestowing decorations; endorsing diplomatic documents, including instruments of ratification; receiving state visitors as well as foreign ambassadors and ministers; and presiding over national ceremonies of state. Government decisions with regard to the matters enumerated are presented to the Imperial Household Agency in documentary form, and the Emperor then either signs his name or impresses his official seal on them. In addition to the documents arriving from the government, the Emperor reviews numerous papers from the Imperial Household Agency, including such items as schedules for the presentation of credentials by foreign envoys and plans for palace receptions and ceremonies.

Officials of the Imperial Household Agency divide the documents roughly into four groups: papers to be endorsed, papers to be signed, others requiring an opinion, and those simply to be read. The Emperor, who is both meticulous and methodical by nature, reads the documents page by page, then marks most of them with small seals saying "Endorsed," "Approved," or "Read." The more important papers must be stamped with either the Imperial Seal or the National Seal, neither of which can be used by anyone other than the Emperor without his specific permission. These two seals were made in 1874 on the order of the Council of State, which was at the time the highest organ in the government. Cast in solid gold, they are about three-and-a-half inches square and weigh more than six pounds each. The characters on them, engraved by a Kyoto sculptor named Otohito Yasui, read *Tennō Gyoji* (Seal of the Emperor) and *Dai-Nipponkoku-ji* (Seal of Great Japan).

Honors are awarded twice a year, once in the spring and again in the fall. Awards of the Order of the Chrysanthemum, First Rank, and above are presented to the recipients by the Emperor himself. He also reviews the recommendations for all nominees for honors, and after the presentations meets those who have received awards.

The Emperor apparently submits to all this paper work without complaint, though from time to time he has been known to smile and say, "It's really piled up, hasn't it?" Whatever other business is at hand, he invariably listens to a briefing on foreign affairs twice a week, and foreign visitors often express admiration for his detailed knowledge of world affairs. Aside from his obvious sincerity and forthrightness, the personal quality that seems to impress visitors from abroad most is his familiarity with existing conditions in their own countries, the obvious care he takes to study a guest's personal record and past accomplishments before their meeting, and the diplomacy of his remarks, framed in the knowledge that any slip of the tongue might cause lasting offense in some other corner of the world. Visitors seem to agree that, though he is never unduly deferential, he is a warm and friendly host. The press, too, appears to appreciate this generosity, and finds him an unusually cooperative subject. He seems to feel that if the press wants his picture, it means the people want it too, and he is usually willing to pose amid the flashbulbs until the photographers have taken all the shots they want. On one occasion, to the horror of his attendants, a flashbulb exploded, showering fragments on his head, but the Emperor went right on posing, completely unfazed by the incident.

Every year the Emperor and Empress spend a good part of the summer at their villa in Nasu and some of the winter at their house in Shimoda. In the spring they attend tree-planting ceremonies in various parts of the country, and in the fall they always go to the National Athletic Meet. Even when the Emperor is away from Tokyo, however, his business does not go nattended, since he has arranged for important documents to be delivered to him each Friday.

The Emperor's work also includes conducting a number of ceremonies traditional within the imperial family. These include the Great Thanksgiving Ceremony (November 23), the Offerings to the Gods in the Four Directions (January 1), the Court New Year's Ceremony (January 1), the Festival of the Vernal Equinox (March 21), the Festival for the Imperial Ancestors, and a number of other celebrations that date back to time immemorial. There is virtually no period during the year when the imperial family is not either involved in some ceremony or preparing for one.

On ordinary days, the Emperor returns to the Fukiage Palace for the noon meal, but when caught up in a particularly busy schedule he lunches with the Empress in the Hagi-no-ma, a room in the new palace adjacent to his office (he usually has either a sandwich or some light Japanese meal such as *sushi* or noodles). Between four and five, the Emperor usually leaves his office and returns home, relaxes for an hour or so and, if there are no evening engagements, has dinner a little after six. Although as a younger man he favored fatty dishes such as tempura, broiled eel, and Chinese meals, but disliked "mushy" food like mashed potato, today he holds back on fats and meat, and eats more green vegetables. When occasion demands, the palace chef—a skilled master of French cuisine—can serve a banquet lavish enough to honor any head of state, but when alone, the Emperor and Empress eat simply, alternating Japanese meals with Western. The menu for each week is submitted to the Empress in advance for her approval, and the Empress herself occasionally invades the kitchen to prepare a dish.

The Emperor, being no avid fan of bathing, usually makes do with a quick dip two or three times a week after dinner, then changes into one of his old suits and, unless there is work left over from the office, joins the Empress in the living room, where he reads or watches television until about 9:30. (For the curious, it might be of interest that the Emperor has absolute sovereignty over the channel selection, but knows which programs the Empress enjoys.) This is an hour when many, if not most, Japanese men the Emperor's age would be wearing a loose-fitting kimono, but he has never acquired a taste for

Japanese-style clothing; indeed, these is not a single Japanese outfit in his wardrobe. Occasionally the Empress, who studied music as a child, plays the piano or sings in her clear soprano, and at ten every night they retire to their bedrooms. It is a mark of the Emperor's attention to his imperial office, and to the health required to make it effective, that whenever possible they adhere to this practice of never staying up late.

Edgar Snow once remarked that among the world's rulers, the present Emperor and Empress are the most stoic guardians of monogamy, and this is perfectly true. In the early years of their marriage, when the Empress produced three daughters but no male heir, an influential courtier recommended that the Emperor choose a suitable lady from among the nobility to be a second consort—something that would have been quite in keeping with imperial tradition—but the young Emperor flatly refused. He was far too devoted to his Empress even to consider the idea. Today, in private, he still addresses her affectionately as "Princess Naga" (not "Empress"—the more conventional form of address) and, in good Japanese tradition, she calls him "Highness."

On Sundays, when the weather is good, the two often take a two-hour stroll around the palace grounds, climbing up to the top of the castle wall to look at the black-headed gulls that have taken up residence around the moat or stopping along the path to examine plants. At least once a week their grandchildren, Prince Hiro, Prince Aya, and Princess Nori, come for dinner, accompanied by their parents, the Crown Prince and Princess. The Emperor enjoys this family gathering more than anything, and he often gives the children picture books or games.

Unless his schedule prevents it, the Emperor always goes to his biology research laboratory on Thursdays and Saturdays. He says his interest in biology began with an incident in his childhood, when he and his brother Prince Chichibu, both still in the primary course at the Peers' School, were summering in the mountains near Ikaho. The two boys were determined to catch a large purple butterfly, and though it took them twenty-one trips into the nearby hills, they finally caught one apiece. Overjoyed, they held a little lantern parade of their own to celebrate.

The Emperor says modestly that his work in biology is not research, but merely a hobby. He has, however, discovered not only many new biological specimens, but gained an international reputation as a "scholar-emperor," specializing in the collection and classification of hydrozoa (coelenterates in the earliest stage of evolution), and often goes out by boat from Shimoda or Hayama to search for them. Putting the specimens he finds in a wooden pail, the Emperor goes through them one by one with his pincette and magnifying glass, grinning broadly when he comes across anything he considers interesting. It is natural to assume that one of the things he looks forward to most eagerly on any visit abroad is an opportunity to meet and talk with scientists in his field of research.

At his summer villa in Nasu, the Emperor spends a good deal of time examining the plants in the area, and when the weather is good, in an open shirt, light trousers, buckskin shoes, and a floppy cloth hat, he walks as much as three miles, with his magnifying glass dangling from his neck. Once a week, he and the Empress take a lunch basket with them and go for a picnic, looking at plants and flowers along the way.

The Emperor has published eleven scholarly works, including *Specimens of Ochisthobranchiata from Sagami Bay* and *Flora of the Nasu Region*. His laboratory, which stands next to the Fukiage Palace, is a one-story wooden building constructed in 1928, so old that the floors creak, though the Emperor is perfectly happy with it and will not hear of having it rebuilt. Here, in his tiny research room, surrounded by books in Japanese, English, French, and German, he works at his "hobby"; an ancient inkwell sits in front of him, and a holder for pencils —many of them almost too short to handle—offering a small reminder of the Emperor's unwillingness to part with anything for which there is still some possible use.

It is thought that there are only two people in the world who have the Emperor's autograph. One of them is an American news cameraman, who was among a group of photographers taking pictures of the Emperor at close quarters as he attended a baseball game at the Koraku-en Park in Tokyo. The photographer simply held out his camera with a piece of paper on top of it, and the Emperor signed it before anyone else noticed what was going on. On another occasion, when the Emperor was on one of his postwar inspection tours about the countryside, an American MP pushed his way through a crowd at Gifu Station and handed the Emperor a pen and an autograph pad. Again the Emperor signed without further ado. It is perhaps a fitting symbol of Japanese-American friendship that two ordinary American citizens possess the only autographs the Emperor has ever been known to give.

The Imperial Line from 1912

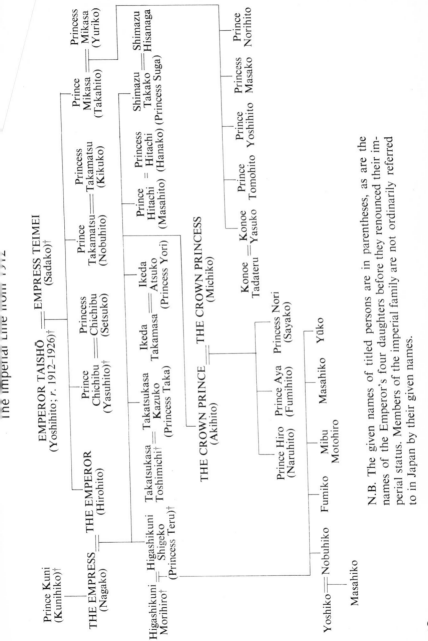

N.B. The given names of titled persons are in parentheses, as are the names of the Emperor's four daughters before they renounced their imperial status. Members of the imperial family are not ordinarily referred to in Japan by their given names.

95